*Faithful Over a Few*
*Seven Critical Church Gro*

# STUDY GUIDE

## By George O. McCalep, Jr., Ph.D.

ISBN 0-9652262-4-7

> *This study guide has been designed to help the entire congregation understand the principles and practices of church growth. It can be used by individuals, small groups, or large groups. It is suggested that some recognition of achievement be awarded for the completion of this study guide. My prayer is that everyone who enters into this study will be blessed in growing His church.*

*FAITHFUL OVER A FEW THINGS* is based on three assumptions: (1) the pastor is the chief catalyst in church growth; (2) there is but so much time in a day, therefore, what the pastor can do is limited; and (3) if the church and her leadership do A FEW THINGS well, God will grow His church.

If you learn to focus your time on those things that have repeatedly proven to be the most essential components for church growth, I am confident you will see their effectiveness in your ministry. I hope you will read the book again and again to internalize these church growth absolutes.

"His lord said unto him, Well done, thou good and faithful servant: thou hast been faithful over a few things, I will make thee ruler over many things: enter thou into the joy of thy lord." Matthew 25:21

God bless you and all of your endeavors!

Pastor George O. McCalep, Jr., Ph.D.

# *CHAPTER ONE*

## Cherish and Prioritize Relationships

*Churches that are faithful over the essential principles of church growth cherish and put relationships first. Building relationships should be the number one goal of the church. The word "relationship" is the most important word in church growth, second only to the word "gospel."*

A.  FIVE STAGES OF RELATIONSHIP DEVELOPMENT
    Identify and define each stage:
    1.



    2.



    3.



    4.



    5.



B.  WHY ARE LOVING SUPPORTIVE RELATIONSHIPS SO IMPORTANT TODAY?

    1.

    2.

    3.

> *The key components of godly relationships are people, love, bonding, and family.*
> *Our definition of a godly relationship is two or more people connected together*
> *(bonded) as brother and sister (family) by the power of God's love.*

C. COMPONENTS OF GODLY RELATIONSHIPS

   1. Why are people important?

   2. How do love and bonding work together in developing relationships in the church?

   3. How are the characteristics of the extended church family the same as any other family?

   4. Discuss three problems that inhibit unchurched people from becoming part of the family of God. What factors in the church family itself make developing relationships with unchurched people more complicated? Pg. 15.

     a)

     b)

     c)

> *The church and her leadership must be concerned not only with seeking and finding, but also keeping and nurturing. Bonding people together by love is the best way to accomplish this task.*

D.  SIX KINDS OF RELATIONSHIPS

Six kinds of relationships must be cherished and prioritized for the church to flourish according to the will of God. Discuss the importance of each based on YOUR EXPERIENCE in the church.

1.  Between Pastor and God.

2.  Between Members and God.

3.  Between Pastor and Members.

4.  Between Members and Pastor.

5.  Between Members and Members.

6.  Between the Church and the World.

> *One of the barriers to church growth is pride. Every move away from pride and concern for self, toward concern for others and improving relationships within the church family, fosters church growth.*

✔ **HUDDLE SESSION FOR GROUPS**

E.  SUGGESTIONS FOR IMPLEMENTATION

What can you do to more effectively cherish and prioritize relationships in your church? Review the sixteen suggestions on pages 21-29. CHOOSE THREE that are within your circle of influence and discuss how you might implement them in your own church.

1.

2.

3.

# *CHAPTER TWO*

## Establishing A
## Knowledge-Based Teaching/Preaching Foundation

> *The Word is eternal. The Word was pre-existent. The Word was with God, and the Word was God. Jesus is the Word, and Jesus is God incarnate. Therefore, the church must be based on the Word.*

A. FOUR REASONS FOR A KNOWLEDGE-BASED TEACHING/PREACHING FOUNDATION
   1.

   2.

   3.

   4.

B. IDENTIFY THE FOUR "GREAT" BIBLICAL ADMONITIONS THAT INDICATE GOD'S WILL FOR THE CHURCH TO TEACH.
   1.

   2.

   3.

   4.

C. WHY MUST THE TEACHING/PREACHING FOUNDATION BE *FOCUSED ON JESUS*? WHAT HAPPENS IF THE FOUNDATION IS FOCUSED ON THE GIFTS OF THE PASTOR OR OTHER LEADERS? ON WHAT IS YOUR CHURCH FOCUSED?

> *And these words, which I command thee this day, shall be in thine heart; and thou shalt teach them diligently...*                    *Deuteronomy 6:6-7a*

D.  THE PREACHING OF THE GOSPEL IS THE *POWER UNTO SALVATION*. WHAT IS THE DIFFERENCE BETWEEN A MESSAGE AND A SERMON? EXPLAIN WHY MORE MESSAGES AND FEWER SERMONS SHOULD BE PREACHED.

E.  WHY ARE CHURCHES WITH A PREACHING/TEACHING FOUNDATION MORE STABLE OVER TIME? BRIEFLY DISCUSS THREE PROBLEMS THAT RESULT FROM A LACK OF KNOWLEDGE IN THE CHURCH.

    1.

    2.

    3.

✔ **HUDDLE SESSION FOR GROUPS**

F.  ESTABLISHING A KNOWLEDGE-BASED TEACHING/PREACHING
    FOUNDATION

Below you will find four suggestions for establishing a knowledge-based
teaching/preaching foundation. Define all four and evaluate your church's
current status in each area. Discuss how you could be more effective in
establishing each component.

1.  Establish the ministry of teaching as an identification label.

2.  Make sure Christian Education is the undergirding ministry in your church.

3.  Create an ongoing teaching crusade.

4.  Remember the power of the pulpit. Is there a difference between teaching
    and preaching? What are the dynamics?

> *Our definition of disciple is one who is a disciplined learner and follower of Christ who teaches another to become a disciplined learner and follower of Christ.*

G. EXPLAIN THE ROLE, IMPORTANCE, AND DYNAMICS OF DISCIPLESHIP.

H. EXPLAIN HOW YOUR CHURCH COULD BE MORE EFFECTIVE IN IMPLEMENTING THE *NINE PRINCIPLES OF SUNDAY SCHOOL GROWTH*. (A one-day Sunday School Growth-Oriented Workshop is recommended if there is a void in this area.)

1. Make a commitment to growth.

2. Identify and enroll prospects.

3. Start new classes and departments.

4. Enlist workers.

5. Train workers.

6. Provide space and equipment.

7. Conduct weekly workers meeting.

8. Conduct weekly visitations.

9. Teach the Bible to win the lost and develop the saved.

# CHAPTER THREE

## Initiate Change

*And be not conformed to this world: but be ye transformed by the renewing of your mind, that ye may prove what is that good, and acceptable, and perfect, will of God.*                                              *Romans 12:2*

A.  REASONS PEOPLE RESIST CHANGE

1.  Identify and describe the three primary reasons people resist change.

    a.

    b.

    c.

2.  When have you resisted change? From your own experience describe an example of one of the reasons listed above. How did your resistance to change make you less effective?

> *People resist change because of fear. People change because of their love for God. Perfect love casts out fear. To perfectly love God is to trust God. To trust God is to permit God to guide in various directions as He sees fit. Thus, change can be initiated.*

✔ **HUDDLE SESSION FOR GROUPS**

B. THE NEED TO CHANGE

WHY should we change? Listed below are three key reasons change is necessary in the church.

1. Change is necessary to reach newer generations of people for Christ.

2. Change is theologically necessary because the foundation of Christianity is the supernatural changing power of God.

3. Change is necessary if the church is to be ministry-driven rather than tradition-driven.

Do you agree with these rationales for change? If so, why? If not, why not?

> *The Christian faith is a transforming religion, and change is central to transformation. We are to become more and more like Christ. "Beloved, now are we the sons of God, and it doth not yet appear what we shall be: but we know that when he shall appear, we shall be like Him, for we shall see him as He is."*
>
> *1 John 3:2*

## C. WHAT NEEDS CHANGING

On page 53, Lyle Schaller lists twenty-one areas in ministry that need changing to most effectively grow a church today. What needs to change in your church? List three ministry areas in your church that need to change, and describe why. In your answer include the most likely reaction to the change you are proposing.

First Change:

Second Change:

Third Change:

## D. ESSENTIAL CHANGES

1. What are the two things that MUST change FIRST so other changes can be initiated? Why are these changes essential?

    a.

    b.

> *Our problem is not a procedural problem; it is a spiritual problem. We need hearts changed. We need hearts regenerated. We need the church to have a heart attack for lost people.*

2. Do you agree that the two changes listed are needed in your church? If so, why? If not, why not?

3. What can you do to initiate change in the members' hearts, and in the style of governance in your church home?

E. HOW DO WE BEST IMPLEMENT CHANGE

Change is best implemented through leadership and creation of an environment conducive to change.

1. How do change managers advance their ideas?

2. Do you know an effective change manager? Describe one change that this person facilitated successfully. How was this change initiated and implemented?

> *Leadership is about change. As someone has stated, "It is important to remember that we cannot become what we need to become by remaining what we are." Also, as I so often say, "Doing the same thing over and over again and expecting different results is dumb."*

3.  Describe the strengths and weaknesses of a change manager. How can you be more effective in initiating change?

    a.  Strengths:

    b.  Weaknesses:

4.  Summarize the first three sentences of the second paragraph on page 57.

## *CHAPTER FOUR*

## Prioritize Expressive Praise and Praying in Faith

> *Rejoice evermore. Pray without ceasing. In every thing give thanks: for this is the will of God in Christ Jesus concerning you. Quench not the Spirit.*
> *1 Thessalonians 5:16-19*

A.  THE MEANING, FORMS AND SCOPE OF EXPRESSIVE PRAISE

1.  Identify the four forms of praise and give an example of each one.

    a.

    b.

    c.

    d.

2.  Using a 1 to 10 scale with 1 equaling "never", and 10 equaling "all the time," go back and rate the frequency of each form of praise listed above as it occurs now in your church.

    a.  _____
    b.  _____
    c.  _____
    d.  _____

3.  What is the difference between true praise and high emotion?

> *People are moved to praise through the preached and taught word of God, the behavior of the leadership concerning praise, and the opportunities provided to practice and participate in praise.*

### B. HOW TO PRIORITIZE PRAISE

1. What can the church do to move people to praise?

2. What approaches should the church avoid in trying to move the people to embrace praise?

3. Identify three ways God's word concerning praise can effectively penetrate the congregation. Note whether or not you have ever participated in such training yourself.

   a.

   b.

   c.

4. Seven Hebrew words meaning "praise" are listed below. Match the appropriate work with the correct description.

   ___ a. Hallal          1. to shout
   ___ b. Yadah          2. to celebrate; rave
   ___ c. Barak          3. to sing; hilarious praise
   ___ d. Tehillah       4. to raise uplifted hands
   ___ e. Zamar          5. to extend hands in thanksgiving
   ___ f. Todah          6. to bow down; bless
   ___ g. Shabach        7. to play the stringed instrument

> *Worship is God's party. God is the audience. We are the participants. Praise music focuses the hearts of the singer on adoration directed to God.*

5.  How can the pastor and leaders prioritize praise through their own behavior?

6.  What is the best channel for participating in praise?

C.  PRAISE MUSIC   (fill in the blanks)

1.  Growing congregations are _____ congregations.

2.  _____, _____, and _____ possess valuable theology that lead the singer to sing *about* God, but seldom *to* God.

3.  Praise music helps the singer sing _____ God rather than singing _____ God.

4.   Praise music communicates to God like _____.

5.  List four positive results of singing scripture to God.

    a.

    b.

    c.

    d.

> *What are you doing in your life, or in the life of your church, that you could not do without the filling of the Holy Spirit?*

D. PRAYING IN FAITH

1. What is meant by "praying in faith"?

2. God has promised to answer our prayers based on our covenant relationship with Him. In the Bible, covenants between God and His people had three stages. What are the three stages? a. _____
   b. _____ c. _____

3. List six things praying in faith will do for you.

   a.

   b.

   c.

   d.

   e.

   f.

Is praying in faith a strength or a weakness in YOUR Christian journey?

✔ HUDDLE SESSION FOR GROUPS

E.  PRIORITIZING PRAYING IN FAITH

1.  How can the pastor and ministry leaders set the example for praying in faith?


2.  Provided below are seven ways to prioritize prayer in your church. Describe what your church is doing or needs to do to effectively implement each one.

    a.  Organize prayer groups through Sunday School/Bible study classes or cell groups.


    b.  Have prayer chains


    c.  Have days of prayer and fasting.


    d.  Develop a system of prayer partners.


    e.  Have regularly scheduled days for concerns of prayer.


    f.  Provide a prayer chapel that is always accessible around the clock.


    g.  Have a prayer hotline.

# CHAPTER FIVE

## Orchestrate Intentional Evangelism and Outreach Ministries

> ### THE GREAT COMMISSION
> *"Go ye therefore, and teach all nations, baptizing them in the name of the Father, and of the Son, and of the Holy Ghost: Teaching them to observe all things whatsoever I have commanded you: and, lo, I am with you alway, even unto the end of the world. Amen."*                    Matthew 28:19-20

A. MAJOR PROHIBITING FACTOR

The major prohibiting factor in evangelism is that churches do not view evangelism as their major reason for existing.

1.  What does it mean when we say "the church needs to break the huddle?"

2.  How did Jesus "break the huddle" after his transfiguration?

*People need the Lord. There is a void in all people that cannot be filled without a personal relationship with Christ. There is a God hole in each of us where only Jesus fits.*

B. THE BIBLICAL MANDATE FOR THE NEW TESTAMENT CHURCH TO EVANGELIZE

    1. Jesus gave His disciples the invitation to fish. What did the fishermen learn from Him in Luke 5:4?

    2. Review the parable on pages 74-76. Do you see yourself in this narrative? Do you see your church in it? Explain.

    3. What is God's expectation for us in "The Great Growth Commission?" How is this expectation predicated on Jesus' purpose?

    4. Why do people in general need the Lord? Why do YOU need Him? Describe how your priorities and values changed since you were born again.

> *From the formation of the world God had a Dream Team in mind to call men and women into conviction and confession, repentance and commitment. The Holy Spirit empowers and precedes. The word of God convicts and compels. Holy people seek and tell.*

5.  Identify the six reasons members fail to carry out their responsibility to evangelize. Make a note under each one that applies to YOU.

    a.

    b.

    c.

    d.

    e.

    f.

6.  Sometimes members do not witness because they discover they have no story to tell. What are the three components of an effective testimony? Why are these components necessary?

    a.

    b.

    c.

> *Intentional evangelism finds a way to overcome the reasons why people do not witness.*

7. Write a concise version of your testimony using the three components listed.

   a) My Life Before (How it was).

   b) What Happened?

   c) My Life Now.

> *Outreach ministries may include an academic center, a wellness center, an economic development corporation, a drug rehabilitation center/service, and others.*

C.  ORCHESTRATING PURPOSEFUL EVANGELISM AND OUTREACH MINISTRIES

1.  Explain below how outreach ministry can act as a "shotgun approach" to intentional evangelism. Describe how outreach ministry occurs at your church? Does it need to increase? Explain your answer. (Pg. 81)

2.  Describe how Growth-Oriented Sunday School (G.O.S.S.) is a very effective way for the laity to be consistently involved in evangelism.

> *The most non-threatening method is to teach believers to share their own testimony. The believer's testimony is not argumentative. Nobody can debate with an individual about what the Lord has done in his life.*

## D. WITNESSING APPROACHES

1. Why is it important that each church adopt one simple approach and presentation to soul-winning? Does your church consistently train one approach? If not, should this change?

2. What do all marketing surveys indicate is the primary reason people initially visit a new church? Explain.

3. Describe why new members are a key component in word-of-mouth witnessing approaches. Are you maximizing this important resource in your church? If not, explain what can be done about it?

## CHAPTER SIX

## Assure and Monitor Assimilation

> *Assimilation in the church is that process which makes new members believe they are an accepted, valued, comfortable part of the church.*

A. THE PROCESS OF ASSIMILATION

1. Who is best evaluated by this process? Why?

2. Describe the process and dynamics of assimilation in terms of a marriage, a revolving door, a welcome mat, playing a man-to-man defense, or life sustaining blood.

3. Identify the four things a new member brings into the church.

   a.

   b.

   c.

   d.

> *God is love, and love is God. Loving and caring are the heart of assimilation. The busy pastor cannot guarantee that love will be demonstrated by all of the members, but he can assure new members that as God's undershepherd, God loves them and he loves them.*

4. Describe the risk a pastor must take in the process of assimilation.

5. What are the keys to effective assimilation?

6. Why do we need to "protect" new members as they are assimilated?

B. STRATEGIES FOR ASSIMILATION       ✔ **HUDDLE SESSION FOR GROUPS**

Describe the major points of each strategy of assimilation and discuss what your church is currently doing in each area to incorporate new members into the body. Where are you weak? Where are you strong? Be specific.

1. Friendship

2. Involving new members in role/tasks

3. Helping people become involved

4. Identification

5. Spiritual growth

C. STAGES OF ASSIMILATION

1. What are the three stages of assimilation? Describe the activities that occur at each stage.

   a.

   b.

   c.

D. KEYS TO RETENTION (Fill in the blank)

1. There are three keys to retaining new members in the church. (1) Keep members involved in _____, (2) _____ of the member, and (3) avoiding _____.

2. What suggestion is given regarding dealing with angry and/or inactive members? Do you agree with this suggestion?

> *Assimilation is important because new members are the life sustaining blood of the church.*

Review the ten steps of assimilation on pages 95-96. Choose three that your church is not currently implementing well or at all, and describe what you can do to change the situation.

     a.

     b.

     c.

E. SUGGESTIONS FOR IMPLEMENTATION AND THE NEED TO MONITOR

1. Why is it important for the pastor and spouse to teach the new members class if its main objective is assimilation? Do you think this is realistic for your church? Why or why not?

2. How can assimilation be monitored? Does your church monitor this process? If not, what steps are needed to make sure this process is implemented?

# CHAPTER SEVEN

## Creating Small Groups

*Koinonia means sharing and caring in a demonstrative way. It is derived from koinonos which means partner, companion, partaker, sharer, road buddy. The best planned worship service cannot fulfill the real need of fellowship.*

A. REASONS FOR CREATING SMALL GROUPS (Fill in the blanks)

1 Effective _____ cannot be fulfilled in the _____ after attendance reaches a _____ number.

2. There will be a _____ that a growing church will reach where the basic _____ (koinonia) begins to diminish.

B. FUNCTIONS OF SMALL GROUP MINISTRIES

1. Identify the four essential functions of the church that can be accomplished in small groups.

   a.

   b.

   c.

   d.

2. What is the one essential function of the church that cannot be accomplished in a small group? Why?

3. Describe the goal of a small group. Are you a part of a small group in your church? If not, should you be in a small group in your church?

> *The best pulpit teaching ministry will fall short of fulfilling the command of The Greatest Commandment if it is not supported and/or supplemented with some small group interaction.*

C.  DESCRIPTION AND ANALYSIS OF SMALL GROUP MINISTRIES

   1.  Describe each element of a small group ministry.

      a.  Face-to-face

      b.  3-12 people

      c.  Regular time schedule

      d.  Sense of accountability

D.  EXPLOSIVE CHURCH TO THE THIRD POWER

   Celebration x Congregation x Cell = Church to the Third Power

   1.  What does the "Celebration" component represent?

   2.  What kind of group is the "Congregation?"

   3.  The "Congregation" is where people know each other's _____.

   4.  What does "Cell" represent in the Church³ formula.

> *The cells must work in harmony with the tissues, organs and other systems of the body for the whole body to operate efficiently. Likewise, from Christ, "the whole body, being fitted and held together by that which every joint supplies, according to the proper working of each individual part, causes the growth of the body for the building up of itself in love."*                    *Ephesians 4:16 (NASB)*

5.  What is the purpose of the Deacon Family Ministry Plan?


    List the three major pitfalls of the Deacon Family Ministry.

    a.

    b.

    c.

6.  How can "yoke circles" make the Deacon Family Ministry more effective?



E.  A JUSTIFICATION FOR HOME CELL GROUPS

    1.  Identify and define four characteristics of cell groups that resemble the cells that makeup our bodies.
        a.

        b.

        c.

        d.

    2.  Why can small cell group administration be called "ultimate delegation?"


    3.  What current societal trends justify the need for cell groups with members that love each other?

> *Even though Jesus spoke at times to crowds, He chose only twelve apostles. Jesus also had an inner circle within the inner circle. When Jesus got ready to be shown in all His glory, He chose only three, Peter, James and John to go up on the Mount of Transfiguration with Him.*

4. Review the list of "one another" admonitions on pages 110-111. Choose three that you need to embrace more fully. Would being in a small cell group help?

   a.


   b.


   c.


F. HOW TO BEGIN A SMALL GROUP MINISTRY

   1. The first step in creating a small group ministry is to teach these concepts:

      a.

      b.

      c.

      d.


   2. How can task-related groups become caring fellowship groups?

> *When small groups meet, regardless of what other agenda may be presented, over fifty percent of the time must be spent building relationships.*

## G. EVALUATING SMALL GROUP MINISTRIES

The Church Growth Institute offers three general guidelines for evaluating a small group ministry. Explain each and suggest strategies for implementation in your church.

1. Total number of small groups

2. New small groups

3. Total number of participants

## H. STEPS FOR IMPLEMENTATION

1. On pages 116-117 fourteen steps for implementing small groups are discussed. Considering the level of small group ministry that exists in your church, choose the THREE STEPS that have highest priority for implementation. Explain what you could do in your circle of influence to implement these steps.

    a.

    b.

    c.

| Small groups will not operate well without effective leaders. |
| --- |

2. What is the primary reason most churches fail to create small fellowship groups? What must the pastor and ministry leadership do to resolve the problem?

# *Closing Thoughts*

*NO PRINCIPLE IS
AN ISLAND*

THE BIBLICAL MANDATE
FROM THE GREAT COMMISSION
IS TO MAKE DISCIPLES, NOT CHURCH MEMBERS!

Teach and implement these seven principles
and God will grow His church.
May the Holy Spirit lead you in all you do...

Pastor McCalep

# NOTES

# NOTES

# NOTES